maker.

D1126016

maker.

Garden

Published in 2020 by Welbeck

An imprint of Welbeck Publishing Group

20 Mortimer Street

London W1T 3JW

Photography and text pp10–83 © Kerry Allen 2020

All other content © Welbeck 2020

All rights reserved. No part of this publication may be reproduced,
stored in a retrieval system, or transmitted in any form or by any means,
electronically, mechanical, photocopying, recording or otherwise, without
the prior permission of the copyright owners and the publishers.

A CIP catalogue record for this book is available from the British Library

ISBN 978 1 78739 269 4

Printed in Dubai

10 9 8 7 6 5 4 3 2 1

maker.

Kerry Allen

Garden

15 Step-by-Step Projects for Outdoor Living

WELBECK

maker.

Garden

Contents

01. DIY Gate

Rather than invest in an expensive bit of bespoke woodwork, why not get out a few easy-to-use tools and really make the entrance to your garden stand out?

02. Rustic garden screen

A stylish solution to make a focal point out of unused space in the garden. This is an affordable project for which you can upcycle reclaimed materials.

03. Fire pit

You will have seen fire pits in style features and on garden blogs everywhere. Pick up a few building skills and create your own multifunctional fire pit, BBQ, and, when not in use, garden table.

04. Tile planter

The easiest way to make a statement with your outdoor space is with plants. Upcycle leftover or reclaimed tiles to make this large-scale planter.

05. Planter with seating

Inspired by Japanese gardens, this seat-planter combo will carve out a peaceful space for reading, contemplation and watching the sun go down.

06. Doormat

An essential accessory for making sure dirt stays in the garden and off your clean floors! A simple, creative make that will benefit both your indoor and outdoor spaces.

07. Rustic tray

Early-morning al fresco breakfasts are one of the many pleasures of creating a beautiful garden. This tray makes taking drinks and snacks into the garden a breeze.

08. Pallet seating

This stylish seating solution is just one way to repurpose wooden pallets in the garden, and can be adapted for any size or shape of outdoor space.

09. Star lantern

Add some sparkle to night-time drinks in the garden with a star-shaped lantern. A make that is deceptively simple and is bound to impress.

10. Storage rack

This mini-shed can be built to protect and store your outdoor shoes or logs, or even be adapted to create a shelter for your dog.

11. Bird box

Whether you're a birdwatcher or just looking to bring a bit more nature into your garden, this bird box is impressive, neat and functional.

12. Living herb feature wall

If you want to get into growing your own produce, herbs are a fantastic way to start. This living wall will give you plenty of space to get your mini herb garden started.

13. Scaffold bench

This ambitious make will test your new skills and result in a bench as practical as it is stylish, and includes a useful drawer for tools and accessories.

14. Storage chest

If you're lacking outdoor storage but want something more attractive than a shed, this chest is the ideal place to store odds and ends, plant pots, cushions, and more.

15. Concrete candle holder

Concrete is everywhere in interior and garden design at the moment. These candle holders will add a touch of industrial chic to your outdoor space.

Introduction

When it comes to creating a unique and individual home and garden, there's nothing quite like doing it yourself. Being able to pick up a tool to build something beautiful with your own two hands doesn't only give you a great sense of achievement, but it also allows you to achieve endless ideas, designs and possibilities, completely unique to you and your space. If you can think it, you can probably make it!

Starting out as someone who is new to DIY can be daunting (I've definitely been there) but once you've learned the basics, you'll soon grow the confidence to try out new things. It only takes one successful project to encourage you to go in deeper with the next. Sure, there may be some failures along the way, and it won't always go to plan first time, but I like to think that's all part of the learning process. Don't give up – keep going. I promise it will be worth it in the end.

Making really is just a matter of practice, patience and a willingness to give it a go. It wasn't so long ago that I was completely new to making by hand myself. I always like to say that if you can cut and attach a few bits of wood together, then you can adapt and build more than you may think. Eventually, you'll be creating unique and one-off pieces in no time, and what better place to begin than with projects that will transform your outdoor space?

Whether you're looking to make something for your space that offers practicality or something that just has the "wow" factor, this book will guide you from being completely new to DIY and never having picked up a tool before, to building something spectacular, in just a matter of hours.

With step-by-step photos and instructions that are simple to follow, I hope this book will give you the confidence you need to pick up some tools and basic materials, and release your inner creativity.

With thrifty tips and ideas for reusing reclaimed materials, we'll be keeping budgets low, so you don't need a packed wallet to reproduce these designs either. Online marketplaces are great places to find lots of the materials featured in this book, absolutely free.

I hope you enjoy the tutorials in this book and that they inspire your own unique take on them, enabling you to build something personal and perfect for you and your outdoor space.

Happy DIYing!

Kerry Allen
kezzabeth.co.uk

Project
01.
Gate

There's no need to hire in the professionals for this project. Creating your own bespoke gate is so much easier than you might think and you only need a few simple tools to do it.

Tools & Materials

Tools:

- Tape measure
- Pencil
- Drill or screwdriver
- Jigsaw
- String

Materials:

- Pallet planks (enough for the width of your gate, plus three extra lengths for the cross-brace)
- Exterior screws
- Gate handle or lock
- Fixings or hinges

Materials tip:

If you're looking to create this DIY on a budget, you can use long pallet planks – they're suitable for external use and are also cheap to buy. Alternatively, you can choose some timber that's treated, so it's suitable for external use.

Step 1: Measure

First of all, decide how tall and how wide your gate needs to be. I'm replacing an old metal gate, so I was able to take its measurements and re-use those. If you don't already have a gate, you'll need to measure the opening where you wish to add your gate. Take these measurements and write them down.

Step 2: Lay out planks

Lay your planks against one another along the floor and butt the bottom of them up against a straight edge. I'm using a long spirit level for this, but you could use a metal ruler or even another length of timber.

Make sure your planks are longer than the height you need for your gate, and that you have enough of them to cover the width, too. If you're a little short in the width, you can space your lengths of timber apart so there's a small gap between each one.

Don't worry if the planks are longer than the height you measured, as we'll be cutting them down later. Mark where the top of your gate will be as you'll need to know this for securing the cross-brace and cutting the arch in Step 6.

You'll also need three extra lengths of wood to create a Z-shaped brace for the framing. We'll add this on the back to secure each plank together to create one solid gate.

Step 3:
Cut cross-brace

For the Z-shaped cross-brace, you need to cut two planks to the same measurement as the width of your gate. These will create the top and bottom part of the "Z".

Step 4:
Screw horizontals

Now you have two planks cut to the width of your gate, you can screw these horizontally across the pallet wood you aligned earlier. One should be positioned around 30 cm (12 in) from the bottom and the other 30 cm (12 in) below the mark you made in Step 2 that indicates the top.

To affix the horizontals, simply screw through both into each vertical plank beneath. You'll want two screws per vertical plank, so if your gate is 10 verticals wide, you'll need 20 screws. Repeat this for both horizontal planks.

Once you've done this, all your planks of wood should be secured together, so that you can lift the gate as one single item.

Step 5: Attach cross-brace

To finish off the Z-shaped brace, we now need to affix the cross section. This will help to prevent the gate from twisting or sagging. You will cut the cross-brace diagonally and affix it between the two planks you installed in Step 4.

To measure the cross-brace plank, simply place a length of wood diagonally across the two planks you just installed and use a pencil and ruler to mark where the planks meet. These are the diagonal cuts you need to make. You can cut along these lines with a jigsaw or just a normal hand saw.

Affix this cross-brace timber with two screws through the top into each plank underneath, in exactly the same way as you did in Step 4.

Step 6: Creating the arch

To make the gate a little more decorative, we're going to add an arch to the top. So first we need to mark out an arc shape. To do this, measure the width of your gate and divide that number by two to find the centre point. Mark this centre point on the gate, about 40 cm (15.75 in) below the top of the gate, which should fall just inside the Z-brace.

Attach a screw directly at this centre point, without screwing it all the way in. Then tie some string around the screw and tie a pencil to the other end. Adjust the length of the string so that, when you pull it tight

towards the top of the gate, it matches the pencil line you drew in Step 2 for the gate height you wish to achieve. By pulling the string tight and keeping your pencil vertical as you move it across the wood, you'll be able to draw a perfect arch from one side of the gate to the other.

Once drawn, you can cut out your arch using a jigsaw. As when using any power tools, follow the health and safety instructions provided by the manufacturer. If you need to gain confidence with a jigsaw, check out some instructional videos online and practise on some offcuts.

Step 7:
Paint and hang

To finish off, I recommend painting or staining the gate with some suitable outdoor wood paint. This will give it extra protection and it'll look a little more decorative too! If your wood is quite rough, you may wish to sand the gate before this step.

Once painted, you can install your gate in position and you can also add a new handle or lock if you want, and maybe even a wreath or house number for an extra-special finish.

Advanced tip:

If you have a particularly wide opening, why not create a double gate by making two gates with this method and hanging them side by side!

Project
02.
Rustic garden screen

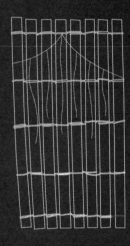

This project is really simple and cheap to make and will add a lovely focal point to any garden. It's an easy way to add interest and style to your outdoor space. It shouldn't take more than a couple of hours and you'll be super-impressed with the result!

Tools & Materials

Tools:

- Tape measure
- Pencil
- Handsaw
- Paintbrush
- Scissors

Materials:

- Pallet wood
- Wood paint or stain
- Screw eye hooks
- Rope

Step 1: Measure

For this project, I'm using wood separated from large pallets. The individual planks measure 10 cm (4 in) wide by 2 m (6 ft 6 in) length. If you can't get your hands on pallets this size, you can always buy new treated timber (suitable for outdoor use) in a similar size from any DIY shop.

How many planks of wood you need will depend on how wide you want your screen to be. Measure the width of the area in which you'll be creating the screen, and then divide that number by the width of your wood.

For example, my screen will be 205 cm (6 ft 8.7 in) wide and my planks are 10 cm (4 in) in width.

$205 \div 10 = 20$

Subtract five from this number, e.g.:

$20 - 5 = 15$

This is the number of planks you will need.

Step 2:
Cut wood

The first step to this make is to cut your timber planks to the required height. Ideally, this will be the same as your existing fence or wall where you'll put your screen. For me, that measurement is 180 cm (5 ft 10 in). Mark this measurement on each piece of wood using a tape measure and pencil, then using the edge of your handsaw, draw the line you need to cut.

Using a wood hand saw, cut along the lines you've just marked on each plank of wood. Always make sure your hands are out of the way of the saw.

Step 3: Paint or stain

In order to give the wood longevity outdoors, it's a good idea to treat it with a suitable outdoor paint or stain. This will also give the screen a bit more character and make it stand out in the garden.

You can use any outdoor colour or stain to do this, just make sure you apply the paint or stain to all four sides of the wood, and apply two coats for thorough coverage.

Step 4: Attach screw eye hooks

Ideally you should position your screen between two existing posts for this project. We'll fix screw eye hooks to these two fence posts, and attach the rope to these to secure the wood in place.

If you don't have any fence posts, you can either install some, or attach these hooks into brickwork with a suitable drill bit and wall plug.

To attach the screw eyes, simply screw them straight into the inner side of the wooden post. You can do it by hand without any tools, just keep twisting the hook round until it's nice and tight. I've used five hooks on each post, at 40 cm (15.7 in) intervals up the length of the fence post. Make sure each screw eye is level with its partner on the opposite fence post.

Advanced option:

Cut the tops of your wood planks at different angles for a more stylized and unique finish. You can also buy rope in loads of different colours from sailing, DIY or haberdashery shops.

Step 5: Thread rope

Now we can start securing the wood in place. This step requires a bit of patience to begin with, but once you get the hang of it, it's fairly straightforward to do.

To start with, stand your wood up in position where it will be affixed. Take some rope, feed it through one of the hooks and tie a knot. It's best to start with the middle (third down) hook to do this.

Wrap the remainder of the rope around each plank, leaving a gap of about a thumb's width between each plank.

Start by wrapping the rope around the front of the first plank, bringing it back round to the front so it crosses over itself. Lead the rope around the back of the next plank, bring it round to the front, and take it to the back once again to cross over itself at the back.

From the front, you should be able to see a difference between the two planks. One will almost look as if the rope has been doubled up. This technique will keep the planks of wood evenly separated and will stop them bunching up.

Keep repeating this alternating method for the rest of the planks until you reach the hook on the opposite end. You can then feed the remainder of the rope through this hook, tie a knot and cut off the excess.

You will need to repeat this process five times, once for each pair of hooks. I recommend doing a "loose fit" of the rope first, before going back and tightening the rope. This will give you a bit more room when it comes to manoeuvring the wood to get the rope around it.

Step 6:
Add accessories and enjoy!

And you're done! The screen should now be secured in position without much movement and should make a fabulous garden feature.

You can also use this screen as a trellis, as it's perfect for plants to wind and wrap themselves around, or you could add some hanging tea lights.

I'll be using this screen as a feature backdrop for our garden table and chairs, so I've added outdoor lights to ours. It now even looks great at night!

↙

**Advanced
option:**

Small hanging
baskets and pots
can be fastened
to your panel
to create a wall
garden.

Project
03.
Fire pit

This tutorial is perfect for the summer and enjoying on those warm evenings. Plus, it can also be used as a BBQ! In the autumn and winter, you can snuggle up next to the roaring fire. With only a few supplies required, it's budget friendly and a project that's great for learning new skills.

Tools & Materials

Tools:

- Bricklaying trowel
- Mixing bucket
- Gloves
- Mask
- Plastering trowel
- Spirit level
- Tin snips

Materials:

- Bricks
- Mortar
- Render
- Masonry paint
- Gravel
- Galvanized wire mesh

Step 1:
Measure and plan

Once built, the fire pit will be fixed in position, so it's important that you choose the location carefully. For safety purposes, make sure it's not too close to any fences, trees, or other wood or flammable materials in the garden.

The fire pit can be made as large as you want, although the one I'm building for this project is 44 cm x 78 cm (17.3 in x 30.7 in). Since it will also be used as a BBQ, I've made sure its size is suitable for cooking several burgers and sausages at a time.

It's important to do a "dry-fit" (arrange your bricks in position without mortar) to ensure you have enough bricks for the project, and to allow you to see exactly how your fire pit will look and fit within the space. For an easy build, I recommend choosing a shape that doesn't require you to cut any bricks. This one will be a simple rectangle.

↙

A note on foundations:

If you're building directly onto the soil, you'll need to lay some concrete foundations first. For this, you need to dig a 30 cm (12 in) deep trench in the area you wish to lay the bricks, fill 20 cm (8 in) with hardcore and 10 cm (4 in) with either concrete or Postcrete. If you already have a good concrete base to build upon, you won't need to dig any new foundations.

Step 2:
Lay bricks

Providing you have a suitable foundation to build upon, you can begin laying the bricks. For this step, you'll need to mix up some mortar. For ease, I'm using bagged mortar that you just add water to. You should always wear gloves, goggles and a dust mask for this.

Using your trowel, lay a bed of mortar onto your foundation and firmly press the first brick in place. As you do this, some of the mortar beneath should squeeze out slightly. For the second brick, you also need to add mortar to either end of the brick before placing it next to the one you just laid. Use the end of your trowel to tap the brick up against the one you just laid, then firmly press down so that it's level with the brick next to it. You can check this with a spirit level.

Any excess mortar that squeezes out should be removed with the trowel. This can go back into your bucket and be reused. Don't worry too much if it looks a little messy since we'll be covering over the bricks later.

Step 3:
Add ventilation gaps

For the fire pit to work properly, it's important to leave gaps between some of the bricks for air intake. The easiest way to do this is to leave two gaps either side of one brick in your bottom layer, where there would otherwise be mortar.

Step 4:
Render

For a modern look to this fire pit, we'll be rendering it. This is a little like plastering, but using cement, and it's suitable for outdoor use. It's also a great way to hide messy brickwork if the finish isn't quite perfect.

It's important to clean the brickwork before you begin this step, so make sure to brush away any dust or debris first. For simplicity, I'm using a bagged render which you just add water to, but you can mix up your own sand and cement mix if you want.

Mix the render in a bucket, per the instructions, then use a plastering trowel to spread the render over the brickwork, trying to get the finish as smooth as possible. It's easiest to do one side of the fire pit at a time, allowing it to set slightly before moving onto the next side.

If there are any imperfections, you can always go back over the brickwork with more render mix once it's firmed up a little, so don't worry about getting it perfected straight off. And don't forget to leave those ventilation gaps you made in Step 3 clear as well!

Step 5: Smooth render

Once the render is firm but not completely dry, take a damp sponge and rub in circular motions over the whole surface. This will remove any minor trowel lines and blends out any imperfections. Keep re-dampening your sponge as you go when you do this step.

Once the render has completely dried, you can use some sandpaper to rub it down for a smoother finish.

Step 6:
Paint

Now your fire pit is ready to paint! You'll need to use exterior masonry paint for this and apply two coats for thorough coverage. Tester-sized paint pots are perfect for small jobs like this and are an affordable way to add character to your new garden accessory. Once painted, leave to dry completely, following the paint manufacturer's instructions.

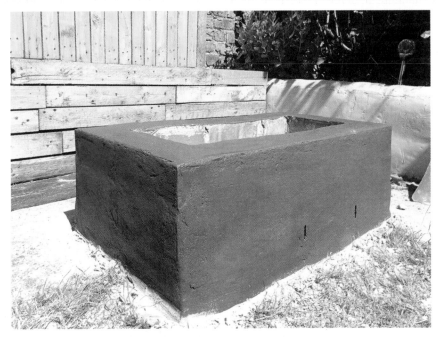

Step 7: Add gravel base

Before you use your fire pit for the first time, you'll need to add some gravel to the base. This will give you a decent bed for burning logs on. You can use any gravel for this and it should be laid a couple of centimetres (an inch) deep so the bottom of the pit is completely covered.

Light a match, as you're now ready to start burning some logs!

Step 8: Cut mesh

If you want to use your fire pit as a BBQ as well as a fire pit, then keep reading, as this DIY isn't over yet! In order to cook food on the fire pit, we'll need to make a rack for the food to sit on. For this, we'll be using galvanized wire mesh, which is cheap to buy and easy to replace.

Measure the inner dimensions of your fire pit and cut the mesh 4 cm (1.5 in) bigger than this around each edge. You can use tin snips or pliers to cut this.

Fold the all four sides of the mesh inwards so there's a 2 cm (0.75 in) edge around the outside. This will stop your food from resting against the brickwork or rolling off the mesh. To use the mesh inside the fire pit, simply rest it on a brick either side. This will keep it off the coal, but be low enough to cook.

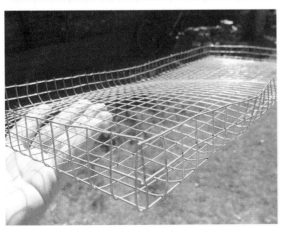

Step 9:
Add cover!

The last step to this DIY is to add a tabletop to your fire pit. Not only will this help keep the inside dry on those rainy days, but it will also allow you to use the fire pit as a table when not hot or lit.

Simply cut some treated timber to size (gravel boards work perfectly for this size fire pit) and lay over the top.

Step 10: Enjoy!

You can now enjoy coffee on the table in the morning, lunch on the BBQ in the afternoon and a glass of wine by the fire pit at night! It's multi-purpose, multi-functional and looks great.

↳

Advanced option:

For a more decorative finish, try scoring patterns and shapes into the render while wet!

Project
04.
Tiled planter

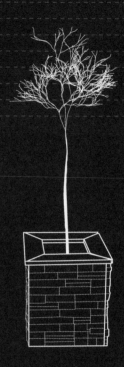

Perhaps you've been wondering what to do with some leftover tiles? Then this project is perfect for you! As long your tiles are suitable for external use, turn them into a quirky and unique planter. This DIY is great for using up leftover materials and you could even make a couple of smaller ones, too.

Tools & Materials

Tools:

- Tape measure
- Pencil
- Hand saw or jigsaw
- Drill or screwdriver
- Bucket
- Tiling trowel
- Tile cutter

Materials:

- Treated timber
- Cement board
- Screws
- Tiles suitable for outdoors
- Exterior tile adhesive
- Landscaping fabric
- Nails
- Wood stain or paint

Step 1: Cut wood and board

The first step of this DIY is to create a suitable planter base that we'll be able to tile. This means it needs to be strong enough to hold the weight of the tiles and also be suitable for tile adhesive and outdoor weather. So, for this, we'll be using cement board, which the walls of a shower enclosure are typically built from.

To make the sides of your planter, cut your cement board into four matching rectangles using a jigsaw. The size you go for depends on how large you want your planter to be. My sides are 45 cm x 30 cm (17.7 in x 11.8 in).

You then want to cut four lengths of treated external timber to the same height of these rectangles (45 cm (17.7 in) if you're using the same measurements as me). These will become the corners of the base and secure the sides together.

Step 2: Screw together

Now we'll secure the cement board to the wood. There should be one piece of wood per corner and we'll use exterior screws.

Line up the wood and cement board for the first corner. One edge of the board will need to overhang the wood slightly so it can meet up with the second piece of board. This will keep the planter perfectly square.

Drill pilot holes for the screws in the pieces of wood and screw from the front of the wood into the cement board at the back, both at the top and bottom of the planter. Make sure you recess your screws so that the head is sunken enough to be flush with the board.

Step 3: Add tiles

Now for the fun part – tiling! Make sure your tiles and adhesive are both suitable for external use.

Mark on the tiles any cuts you need to make and, depending on the material they're made from, cut them with either a wet tile saw or a tile cutter.

Lay your planter base down on its side and, using a tiling trowel, spread a thin layer of adhesive over the whole surface, making sure to apply it evenly. Place your tiles onto the adhesive, pushing firmly down so they make full contact with the adhesive.

Keep adding tiles until the first side is covered. On one edge of the board, your tiles may need to overhang to meet up with the adjoining side, in the same way you affixed the cement board earlier.

I recommend leaving the tile adhesive to dry for a few hours before repeating the process on another side. You'll need to do this for all four sides until complete.

Step 4:
Line base

Once the base has been tiled on all four sides and the tiles are fully dry, the final step is to turn it into an actual planter. To do this, we need to line the inside so that compost can't escape and run away when wet.

For this, I'm using landscaping fabric, cut to size. Insert the fabric into the base and secure it with nails that go into the top of the corner pieces of wood. Trim off any excess fabric – you can then fill the planter with compost.

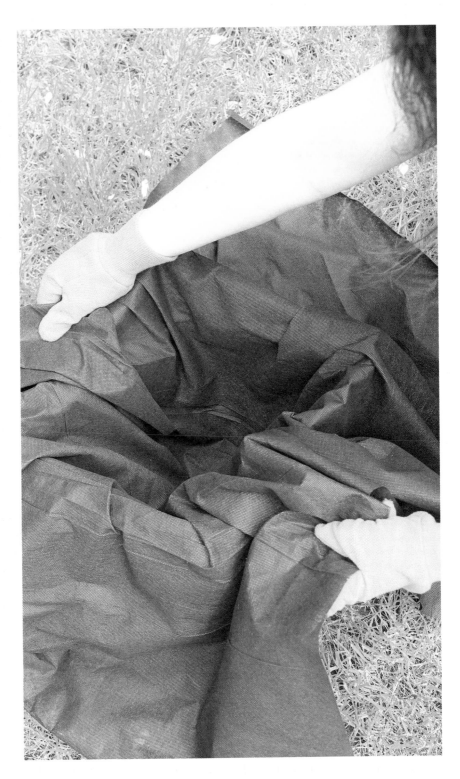

Step 5:
Add trim

To finish the planter off, add some slats of wood on the top to cover the fabric you just secured. Cut four lengths of wood at 30 cm (12 in) long with 45-degree angles on either end. Nail this directly over the fabric and into the corner wood beneath, and it will nicely frame the top of the planter.

You can stain this wood trim if you wish, or perhaps even paint it a colour that compliments the tiles. Once done, add a lovely decorative plant and position your planter somewhere to enjoy!

↙

Advanced option:

Why not use this DIY to create an outdoor table? Instead of filling with compost and adding the decorative wooden top, simply add a slab of concrete to create a handy side table.

Project

05.

Planter
with seating

Inspired by the traditional gardens of Japan, this make combines a garden planter and a seat to create a peaceful corner in the garden. Perfect for a spot of reading on a warm summer's day.

Tools & Materials

Tools:

- Bucket
- Bricklaying trowel
- Spirit level
- Sponge
- Saw
- Paintbrush

Materials:

- Bricks
- Concrete, if required
- Mortar
- Masonry paint
- Wood treatment
- Pallet wood
- Exterior screws

Step 1: Plan and prepare

To start with, you need to plan what size planter you want to build and prepare the ground so it's ready to build on.

To do this, I recommend doing a dry run with your bricks first, so you can visualize exactly how your planter will look and what size it will be. To make life easier, you can also tailor your planter to a size or shape that doesn't require any bricks to be cut.

A note on foundations:

If you're building directly onto the soil, you need to lay some concrete foundations first. For this, dig a 30 cm (12 in) deep trench under the area you'll lay the bricks, fill the trench with 20 cm (8 in) of hardcore and 10 cm (4 in) of either concrete or postcrete.

Step 2: Begin bricklaying

Mix up some mortar in a bucket (I used a bagged product that you just add water to), and be sure to wear suitable gloves and a dust mask. Then, using a trowel, spread a layer of mortar onto the ground in the area where you're laying your bricks. The mortar should be laid evenly so that it's nice and level.

Place a brick onto the mortar, tapping it down gently as you do so. Some mortar will squeeze out as you do this. Lay the next brick in the same way, but add some mortar to its side before you place it down. This ensures there's a mortar joint between each brick. As you place this second brick down, tap it sideways towards the brick you laid first.

Make sure your bricks are level as you lay them, which you can check using a spirit level. You should also remove any excess mortar with your trowel as you go – you can re-use it with your next bricks.

Repeat this process for each course of bricks, taking your time to ensure each side of the planter is level. Don't worry too much if it doesn't look perfect from the front, as we'll be rendering over the whole surface when we've finished.

Step 3: Build support

If you're building a square or rectangular planter, which will have four sides to it, then you can skip this step. If, like me, you're building against an existing wall and building only three sides yourself, you need to add some support at the back to build the seating onto.

To do this, we simply add a small section of brickwork at the back and in the middle. This acts as a pillar for us to use for the seat.

Make sure the pillar matches the front brickwork in height, otherwise you'll have a wonky seat!

Step 4:
Render

Next, we'll be rendering – this is much like plastering, except it's suitable for outdoors. It will add a modern finish to your planter, plus it will help to hide any imperfections in your bricklaying.

Mix up some render in a bucket (again, I'm using a bagged product that you just add water to) and make sure your bricks are dust free before you begin.

Using a plastering trowel, spread the render over the whole surface of the brickwork. Work on one side of the planter at a time, allowing it to dry slightly before moving onto the next side.

If you find the render firming up too quickly, you can add water with a paintbrush to soften it a little. You're aiming for an even and smooth finish with your rendering.

Step 5: Finish

If there are any lines left on the surface of the render, you can smooth them out with a damp sponge before the render completely sets. Buff over the surface until you're happy with the end result.

Allow the render to dry completely before painting with masonry paint. If you need to, you can sand the render down before you paint. I find a tester-sized pot of paint is perfect for small projects like this!

Step 6: Make seat

A: Measure

I'm using pallet wood for my seat, cut to the same depth as my planter. The seat will rest on the pillar we built at the back and the front section

of brickwork, so cut your wood to this measurement. How many planks you need depends on how wide you want your seat to be. Mine is eight planks wide. It's always a good idea to treat wood that's going to be exposed to the weather, so that it's properly protected and lasts longer. I've used an exterior oil for this and applied it with a paintbrush.

B: Assemble

To secure the seat together, cut two more pieces of wood that are the same width as the number of planks you're using. Lay this wood across your planks and, using screws suitable for the outdoors, screw through the cross-plank into each plank beneath. Make sure your wood is attached about 15 cm (6 in) from the top and bottom, so the seat will slot in between your two sections of brickwork and sit flush.

Turn your seat over and pop it in position and you're done! All that's left to do is add some plants to either side of the seat to finish the whole look off. I'm using bamboo in mine, which fits nicely with my Japanese-garden inspiration!

↙

Advanced option:

If you're up for something a little more challenging, why not create a raised bed with varying levels for a real garden feature?

Project
06.
Doormat

Ready-made, designed doormats can be quite pricey, so making your own is a fab, inexpensive solution to add a bit of style to your garden on a budget. It allows you to use your creativity and come up with your own unique designs that will be truly bespoke and individual to you.

Tools & Materials

Tools:

- Scissors
- Permanent marker
- Cutting mat
- Pen knife

Materials:

- Plain doormat
- Sheet of card
- Outdoor fabric spray paint

Step 1: Create design

This is the fun part that will really get your creativity flowing, but it's probably the hardest part, too. Any design you come up with needs to be turned into a stencil, so this means it should be simple enough for you to cut out. Cutting any intricate details may be quite difficult to achieve!

If you're struggling for ideas, then here are a few to get you going:

• A simple star or heart

• Stripes or dots

• Different word designs

• Geometric patterns

You can, of course, also create your design on a computer and print it out, or you can just copy this design, which is a simple "Hey!" to welcome your visitors.

Firstly, you want to cut a piece of card to the same size as the doormat you're using. When it comes to drawing out your stencil, this will help you keep it to scale.

Draw your design onto the card using a chunky permanent marker. Make sure you draw your design in the exact location you want it to appear on the doormat (e.g. in the centre). If you're not confident with drawing and have chosen a particular design on the computer, you can always print this out and transfer it onto the card.

Step 2:
Cut card

Place a cutting board underneath your piece of card and, using a sharp penknife, cut out around the permanent marker you've just drawn. You're creating the stencil for painting the design onto the doormat, so it's important you take your time – any jagged or rough edges will really show up later.

Step 3: Paint mat

You'll need to use a fabric paint for this step and ideally one which is suitable for both indoor and outdoor use. This can be either spray paint or brush-on paint.

Align your card on the doormat so that it's perfectly positioned. Weigh the card down with some heavy objects, just to ensure there's no movement when you start painting. Another tip is to use some sewing pins in any of the small corners of your cutout, to keep it secure.

If you're using spray paint for this project, make sure you go outside to spray, in a well ventilated area, and use a suitable mask.

To spray your design onto the mat, use short sharp bursts from the spray, applying a little at a time.

You'll need to do a few coats of this, allowing the paint to dry between each one. Once your design is fully coated, you can stop and remove your card.

If you're using paint which needs to be applied with a brush, the best approach is to gently dab the paint on with a sponge. This stops it leaking under the card. Again, don't apply too much at once and use several coats until you achieve full coverage.

Step 4:
Dry then use!

Once your doormat has fully dried, you can place it outside and start using it. After you've created one doormat, I guarantee you'll want to make more for other doors! It's so easy and will really make your house stand out.

Advanced tip:

You can adapt this make by cutting your doormat to its own unique shape, or create another mat for your front door with a different pattern. You could also use layers of different-coloured paint.

Project
07.
Rustic tray

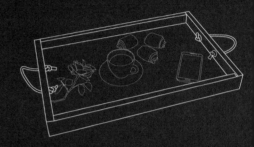

If you enjoy hosting outdoor garden parties or entertaining friends, this is a really useful DIY which will come in handy time and time again. Made from reclaimed materials, its rustic charm will add character to any dinner table and it's sure to impress your guests.

Tools & Materials

Tools:

- Tape measure
- Pencil
- Jigsaw
- Sander
- Hammer
- Clamp
- Drill and drill bits
- Paintbrush
- Scissors

Materials:

- Reclaimed timber
- Sandpaper
- Wood glue
- Nails
- Wood paint
- Food-safe wax or oil
- Rope

Step 1: Cut wood

For this DIY I'm using old reclaimed floorboards, which are 12 cm (4.7 in) in width, but any timber of a similar size will also work. Though if you're looking for a rustic vibe like mine, reclaimed timber is always best – and the most affordable and environmentally friendly.

To begin with, we need to cut the wood to the correct length for the tray we want to make. I used a jigsaw to do this and cut three lengths of this wood to 60 cm (23.6 in) long. These three pieces will make up the base of the tray. To make the sides, I'm using the same wood, but I cut this straight down the centre lengthways to reduce the width from 12 cm (4.7 in) to 6 cm (2.4 in). This is so that the sides won't be too tall, which would make the tray a bit clunky.

With this wood, I cut two lengths to 60 cm (23.6 in) and another two to 40 cm (15.7 in). When laid out as shown below, this will create the entire frame of the tray.

Step 2: Sand wood

Reclaimed or old wood is often rough in texture and, since this tray is going to get a lot of handling, we want all of the sides and surfaces to be as smooth as possible. To do this, we need to sand each piece of wood individually. I've used a palm sander for this, starting with 60-grit sandpaper, then reducing to 120-grit for a perfectly smooth finish.

Step 3:
Paint and stain

To give our tray a little more character, and also protect it from any food spillages, we'll need to paint or stain the wood. I've opted for a combination of both paint and wax, with painted sides and a waxed base. It's always a good idea to use a food-safe wax if you're likely to be using the tray with food directly on it.

Step 4: Glue base and sides

With the individual slats prepared and ready, all we need to do now is fix them all together. Start with the base, which is made up of the three wider 12 cm (4.7 in) pieces of timber. To secure these together, apply some strong wood glue between each piece of wood before butting them up against one another.

To attach the sides of the tray, we'll be using both glue and nails. Apply the glue to the sides then push this onto the base. You can use a clamp to squeeze all the planks together while they dry. Using a hammer and nails, add several nails around 2 cm (0.8 in) apart through the sides and into the base. This will help strengthen it further and the nails can be painted over so they're not quite so visible.

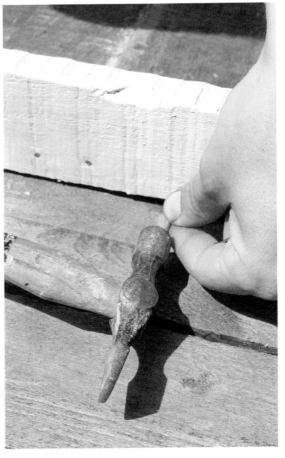

Step 5:
Add handles

Finally, we just need some handles! I'm using rope for this as it ties in with the rustic theme I'm going for.

Drill two holes on either side of the tray, 10 cm (4 in) apart, being careful to keep your hands out of the way of the drill. Feed the rope through the holes and tie a secure knot on the inside of the tray. You can cut off any excess rope with scissors – just make sure your rope is really tight, so your tray is super secure!

You're now ready to host an outdoor dinner party and tend to your guests with the help of your lovely new tray. It's also great for breakfasts in bed – in fact, it has quite a few uses. Enjoy!

Advanced tip:

Why not create a base for your tray, so you can pop it down on its own stand when in use?

Project
08.
Pallet seating

If your garden lacks a "chill" area and you want to add a bit more of a grown-up space, then this is a great make. Many of the makes in this book feature pallet wood from dismantled pallets, but in this project we'll be using actual whole pallets. The finished result is well worth the effort!

Tools & Materials

Tools:

- Hammer
- Crowbar
- Drill
- Spirit level
- Screwdriver
- Tape measure
- Saw
- Sander
- Paintbrush

Materials:

- Pallets
- Landscaping fabric
- Treated timber
- Exterior screws
- Wood treatment

Step 1:
Remove slats from pallets

For this DIY, we're using whole pallets stacked together. However, to save on money (and materials), we'll be removing half the wooden slats from the top of the pallets, as these will be useful later.

Start by placing two pallets side by side, but with a gap between them. Then take the pallet you want to remove slats from, turn it over and place it centrally over this gap. Using a hammer and a large wedge of wood, hit the planks close to where they've been nailed and they should drop off into the gap beneath. It'll take a bit of strength to do this and you may need a crowbar for any particularly strong planks. Once you've removed the slats, don't forget to remove all the nails from the wood.

Step 2:
Plan seating

Choose a spot in the garden where you want to create your seating and position your pallets in stacks of three into the shape you want to create. I've gone for a "corner sofa" type of seat, but if your space is bigger or smaller, it may be worth playing around with your pallets to see what shape fits your area best.

Make sure you have enough pallets for the size you wish to create. If need be, cut some pallets in half to make smaller pallets – this might make them better for your layout.

You'll also need to make sure your ground is level and lay some landscaping fabric over the area you're building on.

Step 3: Secure pallets

To make your seating a suitable height, we need to stack the pallets as a trio. To make sure these stacks can't move, add some screws through each pallet into the one beneath. Two or three screws in each slat usually does the job and when you're done, you should be able to lift the whole stack as one solid piece.

Make sure that when you do this, your pallets are aligned at the front so they're all flush and level. No two pallets are the exact same size so your pallets may not align perfectly on each side – don't worry about this, just make sure the front sides match up.

Step 4: Create backrest frame

For this design of pallet seating, we're adding a backrest. To do this, you need some thick, treated timber. I'm using wood that's 45 mm x 70 mm (1.8 in x 2.8 in).

Cut three pieces of this wood to 95 cm (37.5 in) lengths, or whatever measurement you wish the height of your backrest to be. You can then screw these vertically into the back of your pallets with long exterior screws, screwing into the blocks of wood that make the corners and centres of the pallets.

One of the 95 cm (37.5 in) lengths will go at each end of the seating, and one in the middle. Use a spirit level to make sure these planks of wood are standing straight when you attach them.

Next, add another piece of timber across the top of the three lengths you just installed and secure with screws through the top. You can also add two more lengths of wood between the three upright posts you initially installed, screwing through the sides to secure them. This will add strength to the frame and it will also make life easier when we clad the backrest later.

Step 5: Add planks

This is the part where we'll reuse those planks we removed in Step 1. Simply lay your planks out along the seating with a small gap between each one, to allow for expansion. Then nail or screw them into position.

You can also add planks into the backrest in the same way. Nail or screw them into the top piece of wood and also at the cross-timbers on the bottom. It should now start to resemble an actual seat!

Step 6:
Sand down

Nobody wants splinters from sitting down, so it's really important to sand back all the wood where you'll be sitting – the seat part and also the backrest. You can use any sander to do this, just start with a 60-grit sandpaper sheet and finish on a 120-grit sheet. You'll want to really take your time over this and make sure its completely smooth.

Step 7: Clad base

To hide the pallets on the base, we'll clad over it in the same way as the backrest, but this time horizontally for a bit of a different look.

To secure the slats for this, attach them onto the blocks which make up the corners and central part of the pallets. This means you'll need to cut your wooden planks so each join aligns against this block. Simply screw or nail in the same way you did before.

Step 8:
Build armrest

This part is optional and it really depends on the layout of your seating as to whether you need it. As mine is a corner style seating, I felt there needed to be something at the side to lean on — an armrest.

This is built in exactly the same way as the backrest — three pillars screwed into the wooden blocks of the pallets, then a piece of timber across the top and some cross-timbers between.

You can then clad this armrest in exactly the same as before, with horizontal pallet wood slats to disguise the frame. You can also add some finishing wood on the top of the frame, so it all matches with the same pallet wood finish.

↙

Advanced option:

Why not incorporate storage within the seating? Secure the slats together underneath and add some hinges – a great place to store those cushions!

Project
09.
Star lantern

This DIY is a modern twist on the old lantern design. It's quirky, unique and makes a lovely little hanging prop to decorate any kind of garden or outdoor space.

Tools & Materials

Tools:

- Mitre saw
- Tape measure
- Staple gun
- Pencil
- Jigsaw
- Hammer
- Paintbrush

Materials:

- Timber
- Wood glue
- Exterior plywood
- Paint
- Nails
- Rope

Step 1: Create jig

To make the star shape of this lantern, we need to cut two specific angles with a mitre saw. One of these angles is quite shallow, so we need to create a jig to help us control the saw's movement and cut more accurately.

To make the jig, you need to cut a piece of wood with a 45-degree angle on one side. Clamp this to the centre to your mitre saw and against the back plate. You can now position any wood you wish to cut against it, which essentially "resets" the degrees shown on the mitre saw and allows you to cut shallower angles.

Step 2: Cut timber

With this jig set up, cut nine pieces of wood (I'm using pallet wood) with the mitre set to 27 degrees.

For the next cut, remove the jig and set your mitre saw to the 36-degree marker. Cut this angle into the other end of your nine pieces of wood, using the cut to trim the lengths to 17 cm (6.7 in).

Once complete, you should have nine pieces of wood which, when laid out against one another, create a star shape.

Safety tip:

Your clamp on the mitre is already in use, so you will need to hold this wood manually as it's cut. Be careful to keep your fingers away from the blade when doing so! Alternatively, you could build a more elaborate jig to combat this.

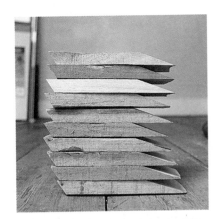

Step 3: Glue

Now we have the star shape ready to go, we just need to secure it together. For this you need strong exterior wood glue and a staple gun. Apply some glue to each cut you made and assemble together. As you do so, staple the pieces together across the joins, back and front, to keep them nice and secure. This will stop your star from falling apart as you continue to add more pieces, otherwise, it can get a bit tricky!

Once you're done, leave your star to dry completely.

Step 4:
Cut plywood

Once your star has fully dried, place it on top of a piece of exterior plywood and draw around it. Using a jigsaw, cut this shape out. This piece of plywood will become the back of our lantern where we'll be adding the lights.

Step 5: Paint and assemble

Before assembling these two parts together, give them both a coat of paint in your desired colour. It's easier to do this while they're in two parts, especially if you want to use two tones like I have. I've used a combination of wood oil for the sides and wood paint for the back.

Once painted and dried, place your plywood star onto the back of your star-shaped frame and nail into place.

Step 6:
Add fairy lights

Next, find some long nails and hammer one close to each of the 10 points inside the star. You want the nails to be secure so they can't pop out, but they also need to protrude around 1.5 cm (0.6 in) so we can wrap some wire around them.

Find yourself some nice fairy lights (make sure they're suitable for outdoor use) and wrap the wire around the nails, mirroring the star shape as you do so. Keep going until you run out of cable. The lights I'm using are micro-lights which work really well for this project as the wire is ultra thin.

Step 7:
Create handle

Finally, drill two holes into the top arms of the star and feed some rope through each one. Tie a tight knot on the inside and cut away any excess rope. This will allow you to hang your star up, whether that's on a tree or a wall – it will look fab illuminated at night!

Sit back, wait for dusk and enjoy your new lantern.

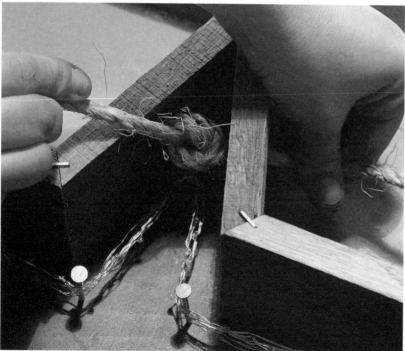

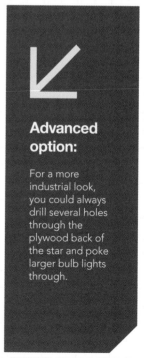

Advanced option:

For a more industrial look, you could always drill several holes through the plywood back of the star and poke larger bulb lights through.

Project

10.

Storage rack

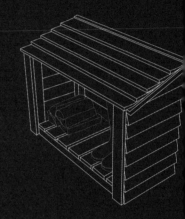

A storage rack for outdoor shoes or wellies is a great way to keep mud and muck out of the house. It'll free up space inside the home and make a lovely feature near any front or back door. Plus, the fantastic thing about this make is its versatility: it can be used for log storage or even as an outdoor dog bed.

Tools & Materials

Tools:

- Pencil
- Tape measure
- Mitre saw or hand saw
- Drill and drill bits
- Combination square
- Paintbrush

Materials:

- 47 mm x 47 mm (1.85 in x 1.85 in) treated timber
- 38 mm x 25 mm (1.5 in x 1 in) treated timber
- End-grain preservative
- Exterior screws
- Gravel board
- Feather edge boards
- Nails
- Pallet wood
- Garden paint or stain

Step 1: Cut frame

Using the 45 mm x 45 mm (1.85 in x 1.85 in) timber, cut two lengths at 60 cm (23.6 in), two lengths at 50 cm (20 in), two at 25 cm (10 in) and two at 70 cm (27.5 in). This will make up the basic frame when positioned, as the photo below shows. The timbers standing up to make the sides are 60 cm (23.6 in) at the back and 50 cm (20 in) at the front.

Step 2:
Cut roof angle

To help the rain run off, we'll need to create a sloped roof. To do this, lay your 60 cm (23.6 in) and 50 cm (20 in) wood on the floor against the straight edge (I'm using a spirit level) and place them 25 cm (10 in) apart – you can use your 25 cm (10 in) cut wood to check this width.

Now lay another piece of wood across the top from corner to corner and mark up this angle.

You can then align the blade on your mitre saw against this pencil line and cut the angle. It should come out at 15 degrees.

Repeat this for both sides, so you should end up with four pieces of timber with angles cut on one end. Don't forget to treat all your cut ends with an end-grain preservative as you go, so they're protected against the weather.

Step 3:
Secure frame

A

Now we have the basic frame all cut to size, we can begin to assemble the pieces. We'll make the sides first, so lay out your side pieces (as pictured, right) then pre-drill two screw holes from the sides of the longer timbers and through into the bottom piece. The two screw holes should be at a diagonal angle (as pictured, far right). Now screw your screws into the pre-drilled holes – preparing the holes like this stops the wood splitting.

B

Once you have two sides made up, you can then add the two 70 cm (27.5 in) pieces along the bottom, to join the two sides together. You need to place these screws so they don't hit the ones you just put in. So this time align your two screws dead centre and side by side, rather than at an angle to each other.

C

To finish off the frame, we just need to add three final pieces of wood to the top. Lay your frame on its side and position a length of wood underneath the top, which you cut the roof angle into earlier. Pencil-mark the cut you need make for this space (they should also be 15-degree angles), then cut with a mitre saw, or handsaw, and screw the pieces in place, again pre-drilling the holes.

Finally, cut another length of wood at 70 cm (27.5 in) and screw this in place on the top at the back to secure the two sides.

Step 4: Brace corners

For additional support to the base, we'll add some corner braces.
To do this, use some off-cuts of your 47 mm x 47 mm timber and cut
45-degree angles on either end. Then affix into each corner at the
base by simply screwing through the front.

Step 5:
Add back panel

Now the whole frame is built,
we can begin to add the outer
panels. For the back, I'm using
gravel boards, although pallet
wood would work too. Cut this
to the same width as your store
and affix with screws. Remember
to use end-grain preservative on
any cut ends, and pre-drill your
screw holes.

Step 6: Attach side boards

We'll use feather edge boards for the sides. Measure the depth you need and then cut your boards to size. If you're using the same boards as me (100 mm (3.93 in) wide), then you'll need eight for each side.

Feather edge boards taper from being thick on one edge to thin on the other. Position the thick edge towards the floor and, starting at the bottom of the frame, nail the first board into position. I always recommend pre-drilling a hole in your boards to prevent splitting.

Lay the next board over the top with an overhang of about 2.5 cm (1 in.) You can use a combination square to make sure each board has the same overlap. Nail this second board into position, then keep going with your next boards until you reach the top. You'll need to cut an angle into the upper boards so they match the roof shape of your frame. To do this, hold your board in place and draw a line on the back for the cut you need to make. You can then either cut the board by hand or use a jigsaw.

Step 7: Create roof

Cut six pieces of 38 mm x 25mm (1.5 in x 1 in) timber to the same length as your store. Lay these across the top of the roof with a 2 cm (0.8 in) gap between each one to create battens. The first two, however, should sit flush, side by side. Secure all of the timbers in place with screws.

Next cut some more feather edge boards, this time adding a 2 cm (0.8 in) overhang on each side, so overall cut them 4 cm (1.56 in) longer. To attach them, start at the front with the thicker edge pointing forwards and position with a 2 cm (0.8 in) overhang at the front as well. Secure them with nails into the battens you just added. Just like the sides, these feather edge boards will overlap on the roof as well, so keep adding them until you reach the back.

Step 8: Add base and finish

Now we just need to add a few finishing touches to neaten it all up. Start by adding a strip of wood at the back and along the two sides, underneath the roof.

To smarten up the front of the store, where you can see the overlap with the feather edge boards, simply add another strip of wood on top. I cut

a gravel board to size for this and it just makes the front appear a little sleeker in its finish.

The final step is to add a base where your shoes and wellies will sit. I'm using pallet wood for this and have left a 1.5 cm (0.6 in) gap between each one, so any rain or mud from the shoes can drain away. Simply screw the boards in place, sand, and you're done.

Step 9:
Paint and Enjoy!

Finally, you can paint your store and put it to use.

Advanced option:

Why not combine this make with the DIY gate (page 10) to create a mini storage shed?

Project
11.
Bird box

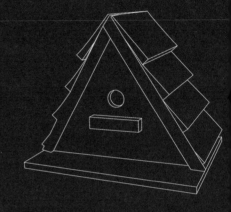

If you want to bring a bit of nature into your garden, a bird box is a really great way to do it! You can be as creative as you want with this DIY and it'll look fab when perched upon a tree or fence. The birds will be thanking you for it, too.

Tools & Materials

Tools:

- Pencil
- Tape measure
- Mitre saw
- Circular saw or hand saw
- Clamps
- Hammer
- Drill and flat-bit
- Paintbrush

Materials:

- Pallet wood
- Exterior wood glue
- String
- Exterior plywood
- Nails
- Feather edge board
- Garden paint

Step 1: Cut pallet wood

The shape of this particular box bird is triangular, so we need to create some triangles first. I'm using pallet wood for this as it's inexpensive and great for outdoors.

To make a triangle, you'll need to cut a 30-degree angle on either end of your pallet wood. The easiest way to do this is with a mitre saw, simply aligning the blade against the 30° measurement. My wood is 30 cm (12 in) long as I think this creates a decent-sized bird box, but you can choose to do yours bigger or smaller if you wish.

You'll need to cut six pieces of wood with this 30-degree angle on each end.

Step 2:
Assemble pallet wood

To turn these planks of wood into triangles, apply some wood glue to the mitre cuts and assemble three planks to create a triangle shape.

Keep it held tightly together while it dries by wrapping some string around it.

Repeat this for the other three planks you cut. Once the glue is dry, you can remove the string and you should have two solid triangles.

Step 3

A: Cut plywood

Place one of your triangles onto a piece of exterior plywood and draw around it.

Then, using a circular saw (mine is a mini one), cut out the shape you've just drawn. You can also use a hand saw for this.

You'll need two of these triangular cut-outs – one will become the front of the bird box and the other will be the back.

B: Assemble

Glue the two pallet wood triangles together to make a single deeper triangle.

Glue the plywood to the front and the back of your triangles. I recommend adding a few nails as well, so it's extra secure, then clamp the whole thing together while it dries.

Step 4: Create roof

To give the bird box a more professional finish, we'll use feather edge boards for the roof.

Measure the width of your triangular box and cut a feather edge board to this size. You'll need eight pieces in total – four for each side.

Feather edge boards taper from thin to thick and are designed to be laid overlapping one another. In order for this to work, you should start at the bottom of the roof and place them with the thick edge facing downward. Then lay the second piece in the same way as above, but overlapping the first one.

To secure in position, we simply nail them on. I recommend pre-drilling the nail holes to prevent the boards splitting.

Make sure you evenly space your feather edge boards as you fix them down. I used a combination square to measure this, and laid mine 7 cm (2.75 in) apart.

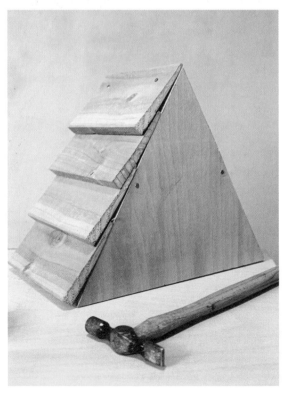

Step 5: Add perching base

Birds quite like perching on bird boxes, so we'll add a base for that too. Place the bird box back onto the sheet of exterior plywood and draw around it, adding an extra 7 cm (2.75 in) to the front to make a platform.

Cut around the lines you've drawn, using a circular saw (or hand saw), then nail the plywood shape onto the bottom of the bird box.

Step 6: Affix trim

Finally, we're onto the finishing touches! To neaten up the edge around the roof and accentuate the roof a little more at the front, we'll add a trim around the edge.

To do this, cut a thin strip of wood (about 2 cm (0.8 in) wide) using your circular saw and lay it in place. You can mark up any angled cuts you need to make, cut them, then simply glue the trim in place.

Step 7: Drill entrance

If you hadn't already noticed, there's one rather important feature missing on this bird box – a hole for the birds to enter through! The size of hole you drill depends on the types of birds you wish to attract to your box.

Decide how high you want your hole to sit, then find the centre point by measuring the width across the face of the bird box and dividing it by two.

Using a drill and a flat-bit, drill out your hole. The flat-bit I have used is 28 mm (1.1 in).

Since my hole is a little far up from the perching base, I've added another strip of wood underneath as a secondary perch. Again, this is just glued and nailed.

Step 8:
Paint

Now your bird box is complete, you can get really creative and paint it. I've gone for a really simple, sleek design but yours can be as bold and colourful or as rustic as you wish. Once it's dried, fix in position and wait for the birds to enjoy it!

↘

**Advanced
option:**

Why not try bird
boxes in different
shapes? I reckon a
hexagon box would
be pretty cool!

Project
12.
Living herb wall

This DIY isn't only decorative, it's also great for those who love to cook. It's a fab way to add a bit more greenery to your garden and making good use of bare and empty wall space. It's perfect for patios, urban gardens or even apartments that only have balconies.

Tools & Materials

Tools:

- Pencil
- Tape measure
- Hand saw
- Sander
- Drill and drill bits
- Spirit level
- Scissors
- Paintbrush

Materials:

- Pallet wood
- Wood treatment
- Wall plugs
- Exterior screws
- Leather belt
- Plant pots
- Garden paint
- Lollypop sticks

Step 1: Cut planks

You can use any outdoor treated wood for this project, but I'm using pallet wood for its rustic finish.

With a hand saw, cut your wood into equal-sized planks. These planks should be longer than the widest part of your largest pot. I cut my planks to 24 cm (9.44 in).

You'll need one plank for each pot you wish to hang. I'm hanging eight pots, so I've cut eight planks.

Step 2: Sand and stain

Next sand your wood using a sander, then stain it with a suitable outdoor finish. You could paint your wood with a coloured stain instead if you wish. These will be visible and a decorative part of the living herb wall.

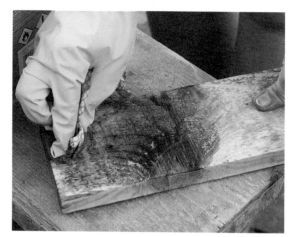

Step 3: Fix to wall

Using a small drill bit, drill a pilot hole into both ends of each plank. Hold the first plank against the wall in the location you'd like to attach it and use a spirit level to make sure it's straight. Then drill right through the wood and just far enough into the wall to leave a small mark.

Remove the wood and re-drill the holes in the wall using the correct drill bit for the wall plugs you intend to use. Insert the wall plug and

screw the wood onto the wall using exterior screws. Repeat this step for each plank of wood, affixing each one at a different height, so it appears "random" across the wall.

Note: You can also use this technique for fences, you just need to skip the wall plugs and screw straight onto the fence!

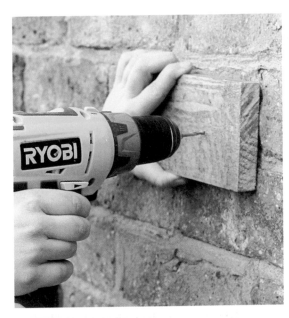

Step 4: Secure pots

To secure the pots to the wood we've just attached, we're using old leather belts. This is a great material to use outdoors. If you don't have any old leather belts to sacrifice, you can often find inexpensive ones at secondhand shops.

Cut your leather belt using scissors, to a length that's a little longer than the width of the pot. Screw the leather belt onto one side of the wood, then, holding your pot up against the wood, wrap the rest of the belt tight around the pot and screw it onto the other side of the wood. It's easiest to do this with someone else lending a helping hand!

Make sure your leather belt is super tight as you do this step. The belt should create a little "pouch" for your pot and hold it securely against the wood. You can trim off any excess leather afterward if need be.

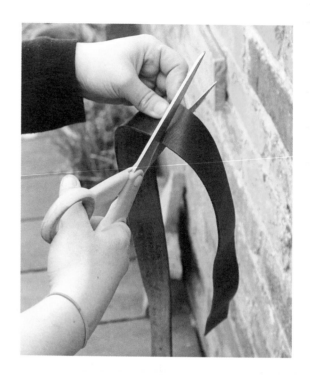

Step 5: Decorate pots

To jazz up the living wall a little more, you can decorate your pots using outdoor garden paint. Tester paint pots are great for this, as you can buy a bunch of different colours without spending a fortune.

Simply paint your pots in any colour or pattern you wish. I've gone for a mix of different colours, a geometric design, spots and even some which are two toned. You can be as creative as you want, or you could keep your pots consistent for a sleeker, modern finish.

Step 6: Add herbs

Slot your pots back into position on the wall and add your herbs. I've added a real mix, from mint to thyme. However, not all herbs thrive outdoors, so do check before you buy. You could also use normal plants for this DIY, if herbs aren't your thing.

Step 7:
Label herbs

So you don't get confused between your herbs, I recommend labelling them. I use lollypop sticks painted with chalk paint. You can then use a waterproof permanent marker to write the names, and pop the stick into the soil in the pot.

Step 8:
Add shelf

If you still have room left to fill, you can also add a shelf. This creates a great place to position extra pots containing plants that you may need to move indoors during the winter months. It's also a great way to decorate your wall and make a bit more of a feature out of it! You can even hang some little hanging baskets from it.

Cut some wood to the desired length and attach to the wall using some exterior brackets. I've used a gravel board for this as it was the perfect width for a shelf, but you could also double up two pallet planks, side by side.

Step 9:
Enjoy!

That's it – your living herb wall is now complete! Just don't forget to water those plants.

Advanced option:

How about making your own decorative and unique shaped pots out of concrete?

Project
13.
Scaffold bench

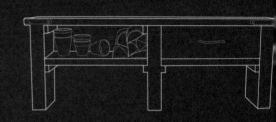

This multi-functional DIY isn't just a bench, it features a clever storage drawer too. What's more, this bench is mainly made out of fence posts and scaffold boards, which makes it a great project for re-using some old materials you might have lying around.

Tools & Materials

Tools:

- Tape measure
- Pencil
- Hand saw or mitre saw
- Drill and drill bits
- Clamps
- Circular saw (or jigsaw)
- Paintbrush

Materials:

- Fence posts (75 mm x 75 mm, 2.95 in x 2.95 in)
- Scaffold boards
- Treated wood (22 mm x 38 mm, 0.87 in x 1.50 in)
- Exterior screws
- End-grain preservative
- Exterior plywood
- Rope
- Garden paint

Step 1:
Cut fence posts

For the legs of this bench we'll use fence posts – they're a nice chunky wood, which makes them perfect for a solid bench. The posts I'm using are 75 mm x 75 mm (2.95 in x 2.95 in) in size, and you need to cut nine of these, each 45 cm (17.7 in) long.

It's important to treat any cut ends with an end-grain preservative as you go, to prevent degradation of the wood by fungus or insects.

Step 2

A: Group posts

Align three lengths of the fence posts you just cut against a straight edge. Use a spirit level to check they're laid evenly, then clamp them together. This trio will become one leg of the bench. You will need three of these trios in total, and each is slightly different.

B: Secure posts

For the first leg, measure the width of your clamped trio and cut two pieces of smaller (22 mm x 38 mm, 0.87 in x 1.50 in) timber to this same width. (My trio of fence posts measured 22 cm, 8.7 in.) We'll use these planks of smaller wood to secure each trio of fence posts together.

Lay the first piece of smaller wood flush on top of the first trio, and add screws through the smaller wood into each of the three fence posts beneath. Repeat this for the second length of smaller timber, but position this 20 cm (7.87 in) up from the bottom of your trio.

Repeat Steps 2A and 2B for another set of three fence posts, so you have two identical sets.

C: Repeat

Flip over one of your bench legs, and repeat Step 2B with one adjustment – the top timber will need to be 2 cm (0.8 in) shorter, so that it is 2 cm (0.8 in) away from the edge on the top left corner. This is so that the drawer we'll be making later on can fully recess into the frame of the bench. This should look like the image to the right.

D: Create final leg

For your third and final leg, the set of two small wood pieces should be affixed in the same way, however, this time the gap should be on the top right edge instead. Eventually, you should have three bench legs which look like the image to the right.

Note: Pictured right, the second and third legs have the top piece of timber cut 2 cm (0.8 in) shorter than the first leg. When laid out as in the image, these two shorter pieces of timber must be facing one another, as the image shows.

Step 3: Cut board

We're using scaffold boards for this bench, as they're the perfect width for the trio of fence posts we made the bench legs from. Decide how long you want your bench to be and cut your scaffold board to this size. The bench I'm making is 140 cm (55 in).

Space the bench legs evenly apart and place your scaffold board on top of them. To secure them, simply screw straight through the scaffold board into the legs below. (You may wish to remove the banding from the scaffold board in this step, or add new banding cut to size, so they both match.)

Step 4: Create shelves

Take the inside measurement from each of the outside bench legs to the middle leg, then cut another scaffold board to these two measurements. You should be able to slot a scaffold board into the gap and it will rest on the small timbers you fixed to the legs earlier.

To secure these two scaffold boards in place, simply screw through the top into the timber they rest on beneath.

Step 5: Make drawer

To add a bit more interest to the bench (and to make it a little more practical!), we're also going to add a drawer on one side, above the shelf we've just made. This will be great for hiding tools away or for keeping seeds and bulbs.

A: Measure and cut

To start with, measure the width, depth and the height of the opening on the side where you cut the cross-timbers 2 cm (0.8 in) shorter. For the height, make sure you only measure to the bottom of the small cross-timber you added earlier at the top of the bench leg.

To create a drawer, you'll need to cut four sides and a base. I'm using exterior plywood for the base and three of the sides, and a gravel board for the front drawer. Using the measurements you just collected, cut your sheet of exterior plywood to size with a circular saw (mine is a mini version) or a jigsaw.

You'll also need four lengths of wood, one to go in each corner, which should be cut to the same height as the drawer you're making. Before you assemble the drawer, you should have something like a flat pack (pictured below).

B: Assemble

Screw the four lengths of wood onto both the front and back panel of the drawer, remembering to leave a gap either side that's wide enough for the sides to slot into. Use a clamp to secure the sides in place and screw these into the lengths of wood at the four corners.

C: Base and handle

Flip the drawer upside down and screw the base into place in each corner. Your drawer should now fit perfectly and slide easily into your bench, and the 2 cm (0.8 in) gaps you left earlier on those cross-timbers should mean the drawer fully recesses into the frame of the bench. They will also stop the drawer from pushing back further into

the frame and falling out the other side. To finish the drawer off, we just need to add a handle. We'll use rope for this, so you'll need to drill two holes about 15 cm (5.9 in) apart centrally on the front of the drawer. Feed the rope through these holes and tie two secure knots on the inside of the drawer.

Step 6:
Sand and paint

Finally, sand back the wood so that it's smooth (this is particularly important for the bench part) and paint using outdoor garden paint. You can then sit back (literally) and relax!

Advanced tip:

You could adapt this make to add a second drawer, creating even more storage for your gardening bits. The top is a perfect surface for potting.

Project
14.
Storage chest

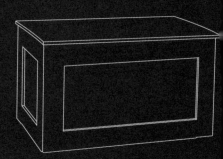

You can never have too much storage space in my opinion, and I reckon that goes for the garden too! This little storage chest is practical and pretty – it's perfect for storing garden odds and ends, and even makes a nice little bench.

Tools & Materials

Tools:

- Tape measure
- Pencil
- Circular saw or similar
- Drill and drill bits
- Hammer
- Paintbrush

Materials:

- Plywood
- Treated timber 40 mm x 70 mm (1.5 in x 2.75 in)
- Screws
- Nails
- Flush hinges
- Paint

Step 1: Cut wood

We're only using two materials for this project, plywood and timber. Our storage chest will be 70 cm x 40 cm (27.6 in x 15.7 in) and we can cut all our timber and plywood before we begin.

To make a chest of the same size you will need 12 mm (0.47 in) plywood and 40 mm x 70 mm (1.6 in x 2.8 in) treated timber. These should then be cut to the following sizes:

Plywood

2 sheets of 70 cm x 40 cm (27.6 in x 15.7 in)

2 sheets of 40 cm x 40 cm (15.7 in x 15.7 in)

1 sheet of 67.6 cm x 40 cm (26.6 in x 15.7 in)

Timber

4 lengths of 38.8 cm (15.3 in)

4 lengths of 54.5 cm (21.5 in)

4 lengths of 31.2 cm (12.3 in)

I used a table saw to cut all my pieces, but a jigsaw or circular saw would work fine, too.

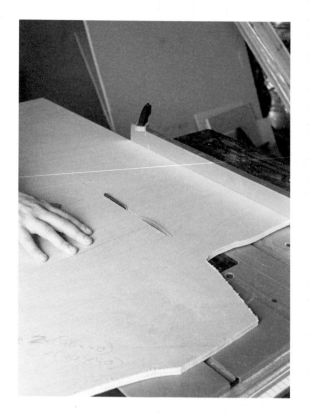

Step 2: Create frame

Firstly, we need to make a solid frame for the chest. To do this, we make two sides first and attach them together.

Take your 54.5 cm (21.5 in) pieces of wood and your 40 cm (15.7 in) lengths and screw them together in a rectangular shape, putting two screws in each end. You need to make two of these to make the two longest sides. It's always a good idea to pre-drill your holes before attaching screws, to prevent the wood splitting.

Once these two sides are built, you can attach your remaining timber to join the two sides together, creating the two shorter sides of the box at the same time. These last pieces of wood should be affixed at both the top and bottom, with a screw going through the centre, between the two screws you installed in the step above.

When you're done you should have a full rectangular box shape.

Step 3: Add plywood

Start with the base piece of plywood (67.6 cm x 40 cm, 26.6 in x 15.7 in). Flip your frame upside down and fix the plywood onto the timber frame by screwing several screws across both the width and length of the plywood, through the frame timbers.

Flip your storage chest the right way up and add the two smaller plywood sides in the same way. Finish with the two larger sides, which will slightly overlap the smaller sides. You should now have one big plywood box!

Step 4: Add detail

To make the storage chest a little more modern, with more detail and structure, we'll create a "panelled" look by adding some strips of plywood. To do this, cut some more plywood into strips 8 cm (3 in) wide. These should be longer than the length of your storage chest.

Cut six of these strips into 40 cm (15.7 in) lengths and glue vertically onto each corner of the storage box, on the three sides that will face outwards. I also recommend using some panel pins as well to secure the strips while they dry.

Once these have been attached, you can add some horizontal pieces along the top and bottom on each outward face of the chest, to create a rectangular outline.

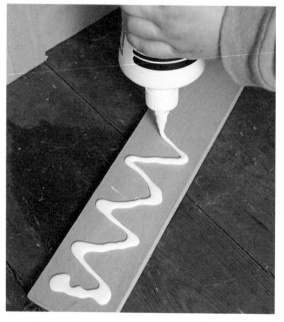

Tip:

You can scale down this make to create smaller storage boxes for your garden shed – to hold seeds, plant pots and twine.

Step 5: Add lid

Take the measurements of both the width and depth of your box and add 1cm (0.4 in) to each of three sides (excluding the back). This is so that there's a bit of an overhang on the lid. Again, cut some plywood to size and, using flush hinges, attach the lid at the back of the box.

Flush hinges are great for DIY as you don't need to chisel out any wood to use them.

Step 6: Paint

Finally, you can paint your storage chest and add any finishing details you wish, like a lock or handles at the sides. Fill with garden supplies or odds and ends, and your storage chest is now ready for use! It also doubles up perfectly as a little seat.

Advanced tip:

Why not create inner storage sections to compartmentalize your chest?

Project
15.
Concrete
candle holders

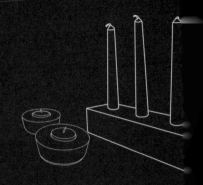

For this project, we'll be using a different material – concrete! No fancy tools are required and you can create this DIY with just a few kitchen supplies and a bag of concrete. But if you do feel like challenging yourself a little more, we've got a DIY to make your own moulds as well.

Tools & Materials

Tools:

- Small bucket or jug
- Wooden stick or something to mix with

Materials:

- Concrete
- Packaging to use as moulds
- Tea lights or candles
- Sandpaper

Optional materials:

- Wood
- Silicone
- Wax
- Candle wicks
- Scented oil

Step 1:
Prepare moulds

....

You'll need a selection of different moulds for this project. These can be as simple as plastic or cardboard food containers, such as dessert pots, crisp tubes or even tin cans. You'll be surprised how many different materials ready for the bin are perfect for this project. Have a rummage around the house and see what you can find!

If you're making your own mould from wood, apply silicone to the inner corners and joins with a caulking gun (this will keep the cement from leaking out). Smooth over with your finger, making sure to wipe away any excess. Once it's dried you can use this as your own handmade mould.

Option: Make your own moulds

If you'd like to make a more specific shape, then you can also create your own mould. To do this, cut some smooth wood to the shape you want to make and screw to a base of plywood, MDF or a similar material. This option allows you to be far more creative and try out some very unique shapes! How about the star shape we made on page 84?

Step 2:
Mix concrete

Fill a small container with some cement and add water to the ratio recommended on the cement packaging. Use a wooden stick (or a wooden spoon also works well) to mix your concrete until it's smooth and lump free. It should be pourable, but not too runny in consistency.

Wear suitable gloves when handling concrete as the chemicals can burn your skin. Always follow the instructions on the packet.

Step 3: Pour concrete

Make sure you're working on a level table, then slowly pour your concrete into the moulds. You'll need to fill the mould with concrete until it's around 1 cm (0.4 in) from the top. Gently tap the sides of the mould to bring any bubbles to the surface. Keep doing this until no more bubbles appear.

Leave for about 20 minutes, place your candlestick or tea light directly into the concrete, depending on which style you'd like to create. If you'd like to use a candlestick, it's a good idea to apply tape over the mould with a hole pierced for the candlestick to sit in while the concrete dries. This will keep it secured perfectly upright (pictured overleaf).

You'll be able to remove the candles or tea lights when the concrete sets, so you can add fresh tea lights and candles as they burn down.

If you want to create a concrete holder for a much larger candle, you can slot larger objects into the mould to create bigger and deeper pits. Plastic bottles work quite well for this.

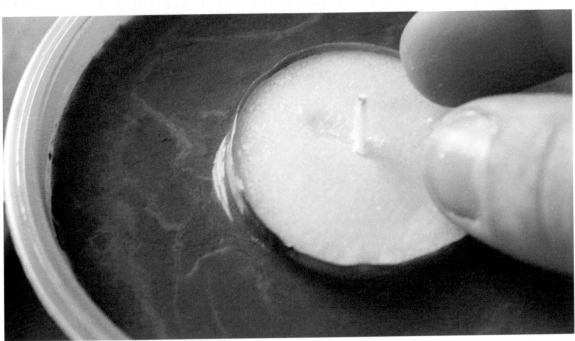

Step 4: Leave concrete to set

Don't be tempted to rush into this step. Trying to remove the concrete from your moulds too early may cause it to crumble if it hasn't set fully. The longer you leave your concrete, the better, but a minimum of 24 hours is essential.

Step 5: Remove concrete

Being gentle here is key. You need to be really careful removing your concrete from its mould, so it doesn't break under force. You'll find certain shaped moulds are easier to remove than others, but if you're having trouble removing the concrete, you can always cut the packaging away.

If you created your own mould from wood, you can remove the screws from the top of this wood, then gently pull the wood away from the sides.

Step 6: Sand

The sides of your concrete are probably going to be smooth but the top may be a little rough in texture. To even this out, give the top a quick sand with some sandpaper so it's also smooth like the sides – start with a coarse grit and progress to a fine grit for a smooth finish.

Option: Make your own candles

This idea is great for making your own scented candles (perhaps lavender to keep the flies away?) and allows you to create a much bigger candle. Even better, you can refill your concrete easily when it runs out!

To make your own wax candle, you will need wax, candle wicks and scented oil.

Melt some wax in a bowl over the stove until it's turned into liquid (or you can use a microwave). Place a wick in your concrete pot, then fill the pot with your liquid wax. You'll need to prop the wick while the wax dries, to keep it upright and central. Do this by looping it over a stick or straw lain across the top of the pot.

Leave the wax to set in the pot. Once dried, you can light and enjoy your own scented homemade candle and candle holders! Concrete is perfect for leaving outdoors, so you needn't worry about bringing these in at the end of the day either.

↙

Design option:

Why not try adding paint to your concrete while it's liquid to create a colourful marble-effect pattern?

Resources

To help you with your makes, here's a list of some useful websites, tools and makers which inspired or were used to make some of the projects in this book.

Kerry Allen / Kezzabeth
@kezzabeth_blog
www.kezzabeth.co.uk
hello@kezzabeth.co.uk

Tools

As a maker, you don't want to be spending a fortune on tools, but you do want something that has a quality design and will stand the test of time. These are some of my most-used tools that have appeared in this book, many of which I've had for years and I can definitely recommend:

Ryobi ONE+ combi drill and sander

Worx mini circular saw

Evolution mitre saw

Irwin Quick-Grip clamps

Stanley hand saw and spirit level

Websites / Shops

Local independent timber and building merchants are brilliant for getting great deals on wood, cement and general materials for DIY. You can often haggle on the price when buying in bulk too, keeping DIY affordable! If you don't have anything local or need something with delivery options then these are my go-to websites:

www.wickes.co.uk (for timber and materials)

www.bandq.co.uk

www.screwfix.co.uk (for other supplies and tools)

www.ukfeaturewalls.co.uk (for outdoor tiles featured in Project 4)

Makers

There are so many amazing makers out there, I could easily write a list as long as my arm! Here are just a few of my faves:

Matt Estlea (YouTube)

3x3 Custom (YouTube)

HomeMadeModern (YouTube)

She's the Carpenter (blog)

DIY Huntress (YouTube and blog)

The Little House on the Corner (blog)

Reclaimed materials

A great way to save on DIY costs is by finding reclaimed materials! Many of the projects in this book have been created with free wood, or from unwanted pallets. You can often find free pallets or leftover wood by asking local businesses if they have anything going spare from deliveries they've received. If not, these websites are sure to help you out:

www.facebook.co.uk/marketplace

www.eBay.co.uk

www.gumtree.co.uk

www.buildersbay.co.uk